HAL•LEONARD
INSTRUMENTAL PLAY-ALONG

AUDIO ACCESS INCLUDED

PLAYBACK+
Speed • Pitch • Balance • Loop

CLASSIC POP SONGS

VIOLA

Audio arrangements by Peter Deneff

To access audio visit:
www.halleonard.com/mylibrary
Enter Code
1069-1501-3679-6712

ISBN 978-1-5400-0251-8

HAL•LEONARD®
7777 W. BLUEMOUND RD. P.O. BOX 13819 MILWAUKEE, WI 53213

Visit Hal Leonard Online at
www.halleonard.com

BRIDGE OVER TROUBLED WATER

VIOLA

Words and Music by
PAUL SIMON

CANDLE IN THE WIND

VIOLA

Words and Music by ELTON JOHN
and BERNIE TAUPIN

DUST IN THE WIND

VIOLA

Words and Music by
KERRY LIVGREN

EVERY BREATH YOU TAKE

VIOLA

Music and Lyrics by
STING

FIRE AND RAIN

VIOLA

Words and Music by
JAMES TAYLOR

HAVE I TOLD YOU LATELY

VIOLA

Words and Music by
VAN MORRISON

Slowly, with feeling

GOOD VIBRATIONS

VIOLA

Words and Music by BRIAN WILSON
and MIKE LOVE

HEAVEN

VIOLA

Words and Music by BRYAN ADAMS
and JIM VALLANCE

LEAN ON ME

VIOLA

Words and Music by
BILL WITHERS

SHE'S ALWAYS A WOMAN

VIOLA

Words and Music by
BILLY JOEL

Quickly, in 1

rit.

WITH A LITTLE HELP FROM MY FRIENDS

VIOLA

Words and Music by JOHN LENNON
and PAUL McCARTNEY

TEARS IN HEAVEN

VIOLA

Words and Music by ERIC CLAPTON
and WILL JENNINGS